A
FISHY
COUNTING
STORY

JOANNE & DAVID WYLIE

FRANKLIN WATTS
London/New York/Sydney/Toronto

COUNTING

First published in Great Britain 1989 by
Franklin Watts
96 Leonard Street
London, EC2
ISBN: 07496 0011 X

A FISHY
COUNTING STORY

JOANNE & DAVID WYLIE

I caught some fish this afternoon.

I asked my friends to guess how many.

My friends asked,
"Did you catch one fish?"

I said, "Yes, but more than one."

HOW MANY MORE?

"Did you catch two fish?"

"Yes, but more than two."

HOW MANY MORE?

9

"Did you catch three fish?"

"Yes, but more than three."

HOW MANY MORE?

"Did you catch four fish?"

"Yes, but more than four."

HOW MANY MORE?

"Did you catch five fish?"

"Yes, but more than five."

"Did you catch six fish?"

"Yes, but no more than six."

"Did you catch seven fish?"

"No, less than seven."

HOW MANY LESS?

"Did you catch eight fish?"

"No, less than eight."

HOW MANY LESS?

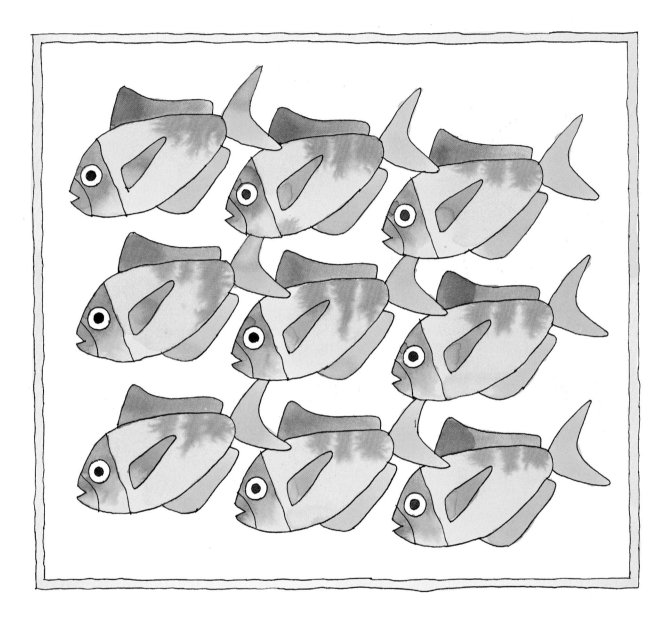

"Did you catch nine fish?"

"No, less than nine."

HOW MANY LESS?

"Did you catch ten fish?"

"No, less than ten."

HOW MANY LESS?

Yes, I caught six fish

and I let them all go!